The Perfect Storm

The True Story of Saving Jamestown and the Founding of Bermuda

Authored and Illustrated by
Autumn Sears Fesperman

Foreword by James Frago

THE PERFECT STORM: THE TRUE STORY OF SAVING JAMESTOWN AND THE FOUNDING OF BERMUDA

Copyright © 2018 Atlantic Publishing Group, Inc.

1405 SW 6th Avenue • Ocala, Florida 34471 • Phone 352-622-1825• Fax 352-622-1875
Website: www.atlantic-pub.com • Email: sales@atlantic-pub.com
SAN Number: 268-1250

Library of Congress Cataloging-in-Publication Data

Names: Fesperman, Autumn Sears, 1970- author.
Title: The perfect storm / by Autumn Sears Fesperman.
Description: Ocala, Fla. : Atlantic Publishing Group, Inc, 2018. | Includes
  bibliographical references. | Audience: K to Grade 3.
Identifiers: LCCN 2018036732 (print) | LCCN 2018043201 (ebook) | ISBN
  9781620235850 (ebook) | ISBN 9781620235843 (hardcover : alk. paper) | ISBN
  1620235846 (alk. paper)
Subjects: LCSH: Bermuda Islands--History--17th century--Juvenile literature.
  | Sea Venture (Ship)--Juvenile literature. | Shipwrecks--Bermuda
  Islands--Juvenile literature. | Bermuda Islands--Discovery and
  exploration--British--Juvenile literature. | Virginia--History--Colonial
  period, ca. 1600-1775--Juvenile literature.
Classification: LCC F1636 (ebook) | LCC F1636 .F47 2018 (print) | DDC
  972.99--dc23
LC record available at https://lccn.loc.gov/2018036732

Printed in the United States

PROJECT MANAGER: Danielle Lieneman
INTERIOR LAYOUT: Nicole Sturk

This book is dedicated to my family and my best friend, Trudy, all of whom all supported and believed in me."

Foreword

For centuries, stories have been used to pass down histories from one generation to the next. Autumn Fesperman carries on this tradition in her uniquely crafted retelling of the epic story of the *Sea Venture*.

Designed for our youngest minds, she recreates the story that played a pivotal role in the beginning of the United States and the founding of Bermuda. This work will surely help form a foundation of understanding and appreciation of this story . . . a story that could have had a different outcome, drastically changing the history of the Western Hemisphere.

It is for this I personally thank her, for taking on the call to complete this very important work.

James Frago
Teacher of History and Social Studies
Goochland, VA

On a beautiful June day in London, The *Sea Venture* was ready for departure to the British colony of Jamestown. King James I hoped for riches, land, and opportunity. The newly designed English galleon, the *Sea Venture*, was on her maiden voyage. She was the flagship of a flotilla of seven ships and two small boats.

"Welcome aboard!" hailed Captain Christopher Newport and Sir George Somers, Admiral of the fleet.

Other important "Adventurers" included John Rolfe and his wife Mistress Horton, Reverend Richard Bucke and his family, and writers William Strachey and Silvester Jourdain.

"Are we there yet?" the little ones asked.

Captain Christopher and Admiral George had
docked in Plymouth, England to pick up an
important member of their crew: Captain Sir
Thomas Gates, appointed Governor for the
new colony in Virginia. Soon they were
underway, bringing with them tools,
supplies, customs, and hope for a new
life in Jamestown.

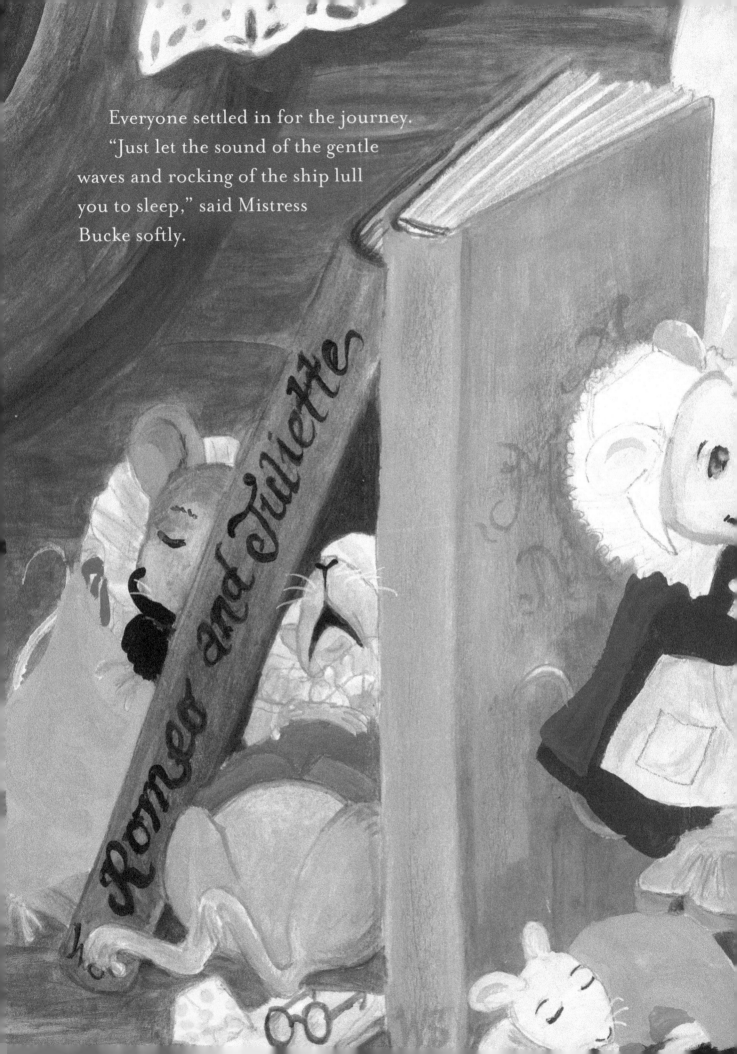

Everyone settled in for the journey. "Just let the sound of the gentle waves and rocking of the ship lull you to sleep," said Mistress Bucke softly.

Romeo and Juliette

Leaving on a mission was reason to celebrate. They entertained themselves and dreamed of their new life. For two months, the ships sailed together, never losing sight of each other as they neared Cape Henry off the coast of Virginia.

With barely a week left, a big storm
awakened them. By morning, the ship was
so overcome by rain and wind, they could no
longer use her sails. Admiral George remained
on the *Sea Venture's* deck, attempting to steer her safely
through the huge waves.

"This is not rocking me to sleep anymore!" said
Matthew, Admiral George's nephew.

Just when they thought the storm
should have passed, it only grew worse.
Morning remained as dark as night.
They had encountered a HURRICANE!
Swells of the ocean grew, and the rain
and wind came down in droves.

Oakum from between the joints of the new ship had not quite set and began to come out, creating numerous leaks. Five feet of water filled the hull, then ten feet! Governor Thomas enlisted the help of every member on board, bailing out or working the pump, to stay afloat!

On the fourth day of the storm, clouds
began to part and Admiral George navigated
the ship's position. Not another ship of the flotilla
was in sight. Did they survive the storm? Hungry and
exhausted, fear set in.

They had survived a hurricane,
but they were still sinking.

"We cannot hold over ten feet of water in our hull; we must lighten the ship!" shouted Governor Thomas.

"Toss over your luggage! Toss over liquids such as oils, cider, and vinegar! Toss over the cannons!" he continued.

On the fifth day, Admiral George spent every minute navigating, steering, and searching the horizon.

"Land!" he cried.

It was the Isles de Bermudez, now called Bermuda.
Superstitious sailors had dubbed it the "Isle of Devils," but it
was not as feared as the bottom of the ocean!

With expert knowledge of the islands' reefs, Admiral George
purposely guided and wedged the *Sea Venture* between rocks,
preventing her from sinking.

All 150 passengers, including the ship's dog, arrived safely
on the beach.

The *Sea Venture* remained above the waves where supplies and tools could be removed for use.

The island was not as scary as imagined. The howling noises were the native cahow bird that was easy to catch for food. A few caves even had a little fresh water.

"Tell me about the new colony again?" Admiral George's nephew asked with a yawn.

The castaways found many more resources on the islands that would help them: large cedar trees, palms, mulberries, limestone, and prickley pears they could eat.

Wild boar was also found, possibly left from previous shipwrecks where they swam to shore.

Birds, fish, lobster, and sea turtles
were plentiful and easy to catch.

"I caught a fish!"

"I caught a sea star!"

"I caught a . . . um . . . a . . . ?"
said Matthew.

Governor Thomas began construction of a new ship, using masts and beams salvaged from the *Sea Venture*. Admiral George built a small boat and used it to map the islands. He also hunted and caught enough fish to keep everyone fed.

"Can I keep him?" asked Matthew.

Governor Thomas made good progress building a new ship; he named her *Deliverance*. It had been two months, and no other ships had arrived from Virginia or England to help them.

"We need a second ship to fit everyone and supplies," he told Governor Thomas, "And I can build it!"

Governor Thomas was thankful. He shared his supply of tools, workers, and salvaged ship parts. Much of the timber from the shipwrecked *Sea Venture* was already used to build the *Deliverance*, so Admiral George built his ship mostly of local cedar. He named her *Patience*.

Admiral George planted a garden where Governor Thomas had first set foot on land above the beach. Some seeds brought from England were successful and some were not.

"Awwwww, onions and potatoes? I wanted watermelons!"
sulked Matthew.

A few items were stored to bring to the colony, but the state of the colony was unknown. With a final look at the bountiful and beautiful islands of Bermuda, Governor Thomas built a monument in Admiral George's garden. He fashioned two timbers from the shipwrecked *Sea Venture* into a cross and mounted it sturdily to a cedar. He attached a 12-pence coin with King James I in the center and inscribed the following:

"In memory of our great deliverance, both from a mighty storm and leak, we have set up this to the honor of God. It is the spoil of an English ship called the 'Sea Venture', bound with seven ships more to Virginia, or Nova Britannia, in America. In it were two knights, Sir Thomas Gates, Knight, governor of the English forces and colony there, and Sir George Somers, Knight, admiral of the seas. Her captain was Christopher Newport; passengers and mariners she had beside one hundred and fifty. We were forced to run her ashore under a point that bore southeast from the northern point of the island, which we discovered first the eight-and-twentieth of July, 1609."

Many considered staying on the islands.
Although they once feared it, plentiful
resources and a milder climate quickly appealed
to the castaways. These 'adventurers' had a
mission, however: to assist the development
of Jamestown for the investors of the Virginia
Company and King James I. Only a few
remained in Bermuda. The rest boarded the
two new ships, *Deliverance* and *Patience*, and
set out to complete their journey across the
Atlantic Ocean.

It took two weeks to arrive at the Jamestown colony. It was spring, just after "the starving time" of winter. All of the ships from the flotilla had arrived except one small ship. Looking for family and friends, they found only 60 colonists remained of the original 400.

Relations with local natives, Powhatan Indians, were hostile, and morale was low. The entire colony had fallen into illness, idleness, and disrepair. Governor Thomas shared supplies with the starving colonists and reported the sad state of affairs to his passengers.

Seeds had not been planted. Gardens
had not been tended. Chickens, pigs,
and local deer had all been killed or
driven away by the Powhatan. Even
fishing further downstream could not
gather enough fish.

With just two weeks of rations left, Governor Thomas
assisted the remaining colonists in boarding ships to take them
north to Nova Brittania and make their way back to England.

"Hey, is that a boat?" asked someone.

Halfway down the James River, Lord Thomas La Warr's
company of three supply ships came into view.

"That means FOOD!" cheered Matthew.

Everyone headed back up the
James River to settle Jamestown with
fresh workers and additional supplies.
Governor La Warr had arrived to replace
Governor Thomas. Working together,
they brought the Jamestown colony back
from the brink of disaster.

Admiral George volunteered to return to Bermuda to
gather wild boar, birds, fish, and supplies to bring back.
After all, Bermuda reefs were dangerous — and he knew
them better than anyone.

"You can decide what's for dinner, Matthew," said his uncle. "You have the choice of fish, fish, or fish!"

Accompanied by his nephew, Admiral George navigated to Bermuda safely yet again, following his heart's desire to bountiful and beautiful Bermuda.

The End

Find the Hidden Treasure

These artifacts are featured within the story. They are exhibited by The National Museum of Bermuda at Dockyard. The Queen's Gallery houses the exhibit "Shipwreck Island: Sunken Clues to Bermuda's Past", where the featured items may be viewed.

Can you spot them within the story?

Somer's Map

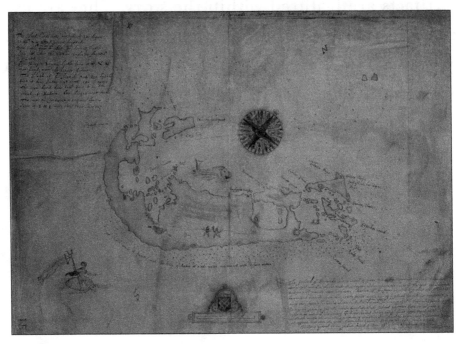

This map was originally drawn by Admiral Sir George Somers whilst shipwrecked and building 2 new ships to carry the survivors to Virginia. Permission for printing of this map has been granted by the Bermuda National Trust.

Norwood Map

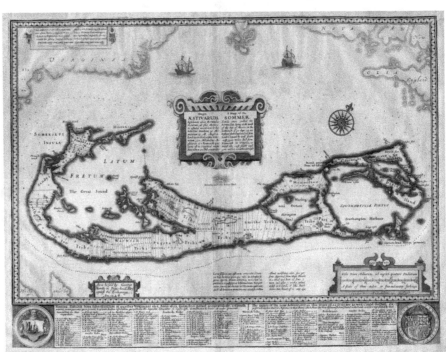

Glossary

Adventurer: name given to colonists invested in the Virginia Company, including those who pay passage on ships traveling to the new colony

artifact: a usually simple object used and modified by humans, such as a tool or ornament

Deliverance: name given to the ship built in Bermuda by Governor Sir Thomas Gates, meaning to be delivered, liberated, or rescued from something

flagship: the finest, largest, or most important one of a group of things; the ship that carries the commander of a fleet or subdivision of a fleet and flies the commander's flag

flotilla: a fleet of ships or boats

navigate: to steer a course on, over, or through

Patience: Name given to the ship built in Bermuda by Admiral Sir George Somers, meaning the capacity, habit, or fact of being patient.

Powhatan-Wahunsonacock (*Wa-hun-sen-a-cawh*): name given by colonists to native people found in area of the Jamestown Colony

reef: a chain of rocks or coral, or a ridge of sand at or near the surface of water that can cause damage to ships

"Starving time": winter of 1609-1610 at the Jamestown Colony when colonists had little or no food

victual: supplies of food.

Virginia Company: collection of investors in London, England whose mission was to supply and colonize new lands

Author's Endnotes

Many stories in history have been lost forever. Occasionally, a source is found and a story comes to light that was lost, illuminating facts that change our understanding of what we thought happened. There are also many sides of a story. Artifacts left behind and firsthand accounts give us valuable information.

Marine archaeology has made significant technological advances, providing additional clues to complete a story. In the case of the *Sea Venture*, firsthand accounts, artifacts recovered from the shipwreck, shipwright's notes from England, and current technological advances in computer modeling and testing have all been brought together to formulate a complete story. It is the "Perfect Storm" of sources to assemble a true account.

The artifacts of the *Sea Venture* featured in this story are items passengers left behind after the ship was set into the reefs. They cleared what they could from the ship, including supplies, tools, personal belongings, rigging, and parts. Although we know what items were used for, we cannot necessarily identify an item's specific owner. It is of great mystery and curiosity to me who owned the items.

Who lost a gold friendship ring? Everyone survived the shipwreck, so was it stashed away for giving? Or had someone set it aside for safekeeping after receiving it previously from an admirer? Perhaps a young sailor brought it with him from England in the hope of one day finding a wife in the new colony.

A large scabbard hilt was found completely engulfed in coral. Was it dropped down into the ship where it couldn't be reached?

Did someone lose it while attempting to gather supplies or parts from the half-sunk ship?

What about the tiny gold crucifix? Did it drop from a pocket or necklace into the creases of the ship floor while working at bailing out water during the hurricane?

Although no tools and few items were left behind on the *Sea Venture*, we can accept with reasonable assurance that items common to this time period would likely have been used. Similar items found on the shipwrecked *Warwick*, of the same time period, sunk unexpectedly in 1619 while tied off in Castle Harbor during a hurricane. Tools used by Sir Thomas Gates in "The Perfect Storm" are modeled after tools recovered from the *Warwick* shipwreck.

Acknowledgements

This children's' picture book is based on a true story, from accounts of the Shipwreck of the *Sea Venture* and its role in the redemption of Jamestown:

"*A Voyage to Virginia in 1609*" Two Narratives Strachey's 'True Reportory' & Jourdain's '*Discovery of the Bermudas*' Edited by Louis B. Wright

Published for the Association for the Preservation of Virginia Antiquities, The University Press of Virginia Published with the assistance of the Jamestown Foundation Copyright 1964 by the Rector and Visitors of the University of Virginia Published 1964, 1965, 1967

Library of Congress Catalog Card Number: 64-19202 Printed in the United States of America by The Dietz Press, Inc.

This children's' book was also inspired by and references information in the documentary film, "Downing's Wreck" by Look-Bermuda Productions.
    https://www.lookbermuda.com/

Map of Bermuda drawn in 1609 by Sir George Somers

Webpage link to National Museum of Bermuda:
    https://nmb.bm

Webpage link to Bermuda Underwater Exploration Institute
    http://www.buei.bm

Webpage link to LookBermuda for viewing documentary, "Downing's Wreck"

    https://lookbermuda.com

    https://lookbermuda.com/seaventure

Glossary for teachers and students

Old world map of Atlantic including Jamestown, Bermuda, and England for end papers, Drawn by John Speed, based on previous map by Richard Norwood in 1626.

Foreword:

Mr. James Frago, History Teacher, Goochland County Public Schools, Virginia

---

Artifact photos from National Museum of Bermuda:

Special thank you to Jane Downing, Registrar, National Museum of Bermuda and Edmund Downing/Sir Thomas Gates descendant, for her extraordinary assistance. Her expert consultation regarding usage of artifacts within "The Perfect Storm", as well as providing numerous photos and maps, has made this telling of Bermuda's story possible.

Autumn Fesperman has always been drawn to books, animals, drawing, and the ocean. Moving around in a Navy family provided for lots of experiences to draw and write about. She currently resides in Virginia with her family of 6 and 2 lazy cats and teaches middle school art. During the summer, she travels to Bermuda, where she loves to research, write, draw, and paint in between going to the beach and snorkeling. Visit autumnfesperman.com to see more of her work.

CPSIA information can be obtained
at www.ICGtesting.com
Printed in the USA
FFHW012114141218
49834194-54387FF